From Maintenance to Mission

Towards the Conversion of England Too

Paul Simmonds

Formerly Head of Adult Training and Resources, CPAS and now
the Mission Adviser for the Coventry Diocese and continuing on
the staff of St Margaret's Parish Church, Wolston

GROVE BOOKS LIMITED

RIDLEY HALL RD CAMBRIDGE CB3 9HU

Contents

Acknowledgements

This booklet has been influenced by countless conversations and meetings with a whole variety of local church ministers and lay leaders, who have been trying to discern the way forward for the church. In my work at CPAS I have had the privilege of being exposed to the thinking of some influential thinkers and practitioners in the field of mission. This booklet is inspired by them. I therefore want to thank all of them and my CPAS colleagues who for the past thirteen years have kept 'mission at home,' as we used to call it, on my agenda.

Many of the principles discussed here have been talked about at St Margaret's, Wolston, a village church of around a hundred members, where I have been honorary curate for six years and where I am now a part-time stipendiary minister. I want to thank them for being guinea pigs for a variety of ideas and suggestions from 'seeker services' to 'cell churches.'

The Cover Illustration is by a member of our Pathfinder group

First Impression November 1995
ISSN 0953-4946
ISBN 1 85174 304 9

1
From Maintenance to Mission—Why?

'There can be no doubt that there is a wide and deep gulf between the Church and the people...'

'The present irrelevance of the Church in the life and thought of the community in general is apparent from two symptoms which admit of no dispute. They are (1) the widespread decline in church going; and (2) the collapse of Christian moral standards...'

'It is indisputable that only a small percentage of the nation today joins regularly in public worship of any kind.'[1]

Are these statements the result of a recent survey or yet another press report of church decline? No, they were published fifty years ago in 1945, in the report 'Towards the Conversion of England.' You might think that such a report would have resulted in a special group to lead the church in a new direction in mission. The extraordinary thing about it is that almost nothing was done to implement this report. It took twenty years to appoint a council for evangelism, and it was even later that the Church of England appointed an officer for evangelism. But the challenge is still largely unmet. There has been steady decline in church attendance since that time; indeed the situation has become far more serious.

According to Robin Greenwood, 'for the majority of people in this country our churches are irrelevant, peripheral and seemingly only concerned with their own trivial pursuits.'[2] Robert Warren himself comments, 'No commercial operation would have waited as long as the Church of England has done before developing a corporate strategy to deal with the situation. Yes, the church is more than a corporate structure—but it is not less than one.'

Towards the Conversion of England was strong on analysis and bold in some of its suggestions. So why was it ignored? I think there are several reasons. The first was that the institution of the church was simply not prepared to change. The second was that the church was cushioned from reality by its inherited financial resources. Perhaps there was a third. In a time that followed such widespread upheaval, church people preferred the church to concentrate on its traditional pastoral role, offering some stability in a rapidly changing world. They opted to keep the church as they liked it even if that meant keeping it to themselves.

The situation has changed in regard to all three. First, the Turnbull report[3] is evidence of the church's realisation that radical structural change is needed. Second, the church is having to create a new financial base, relying on present members

---

1   *Towards the Conversion of England*, 1945.
2   *Reclaiming the Church*, p 156, quoted by Robert Warren in *Building Missionary Congregations*.
3   *Working as One Body* (London: Church House Publishing, October 1995).

not past benefactors. Third, while there is a strong dependency on the church as a spiritual base in a time of change, there is, I believe, a growing conviction that the church has to change for the purpose of mission.

The Search for Growth

Church leaders in the last ten years have been searching with growing intensity for ways to halt the decline in numbers and to initiate a new period of confident faith sharing. There have been plenty of individual churches which are growing. Overall however, the rate of growth is too slow. The loss of members, especially to join the ranks of the church triumphant, mean that overall there is no significant numerical church growth in the Church of England at the moment

A lot of effective evangelism has been done by church members and leaders. There has been a constant flow of fresh thinking and new ideas coming their way. This is a healthy sign. The church is more open to change now than at any time that I can remember. At times people have been tempted to shout 'Eureka!' as the church has made fresh discoveries and created valuable new approaches—Toronto, Adult Catechumenate, DAWN, Audits, Willow Creek, Thomas Mass, Church Growth, Cursillo, Alpha, Meta Church, Holy Disorder, Church Planting, Gospel and Culture, and Power Evangelism to name but a few (apologies if I have left out your 'eureka').

Many of these new approaches have made a substantial impact on some churches. But there is always the danger of looking for what I call the 'clincher,' that one principle, model or spiritual insight which will turn the church around. I do not think it exists. However, the church is coming, with an increasing sense of unanimity, to a realisation that there is an essential step that it has to take. It is not of itself a clincher, but it is a huge change. Unless we take this step, decline will be rapid and probably fatal for the Church of England. There is wide agreement on two points. Firstly, current numerical growth in individual churches is not sufficient to ensure substantial net growth overall. And secondly, any substantial numerical growth is not sustainable with the present way of 'doing' church.

Most congregations are not structured to cope with an influx of new people. The church we have *inherited* was designed to maintain and pastor a Christian population. The church which needs to *emerge* will be a missionary church designed to help the Christian minority to evangelize the nation and work, 'towards the conversion of England.' We need what Robert Warren has called *missionary congregations*. As he has gone round the country describing his conclusions people are saying: 'Yes, that is exactly right, this is the fundamental change we need.'

Make no mistake, it is a huge change—a 'paradigm shift' or change in approach. No one knows what will emerge. No one knows quite what missionary congregations from Dockland to Fenland will look like. It is exciting and it is awesome. But I cannot emphasize too strongly that what we are talking about does not yet exist. We have plenty of evangelism bolted on to predominantly pastoral churches. The initiatives listed earlier also form part of the picture. They are important pieces of the jigsaw—but the complete jigsaw does not yet exist.

A Picture of History

For me, the need for a missionary congregation can be seen most clearly by looking at the history of the church. Reducing the last two thousand years of church history into a simple graph, we can see the situation clearly.

The New Testament church was undoubtedly a missionary church. It was lightweight on organisation with little institutional baggage. Above all, it took the great commission (to 'make disciples of all nations') and fulfilled it across many nations, until Christianity became established and the church moved from a missionary to a maintenance footing. Robert Warren comments that 'The church in "pastoral mode" is a church in a Christendom setting where the vast majority of the population are baptized and, notionally at least, Christian. Such a culture can be described as "Christian" because the values and worldview of that culture stem from Christian roots.'[4]

The structures of the Church of England were institutionalized at a time when the church was no longer in missionary mode. So everything from Rural Deans to the concept of the parish as the 'cure of souls' stemmed from this age. It was designed for that situation. We search in vain in the 1662 Prayer Book for any obvious reference to evangelism. It was a Christian society. Liturgically, structurally, legally and of course in relation to buildings and ministry, the church has continued to operate in this historic pastoral mode.

Yet the rest of the world has changed. As far as England is concerned, we are

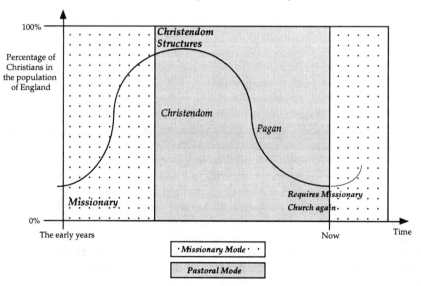

Diagrammatic representation of the rise and fall in proportion of Christians in the population of England since the coming of Christianity.

---

4   Robert Warren, *Building Missionary Congregations* (London: Church House Publishing) p 3.

increasingly a pagan society—the 1945 report already spoke of the 'pagan atmosphere.' We are in need of a missionary church rather than a pastoral church. That is not to say the missionary church will not pastor—that is clearly not the case. The pastoral epistles were written to a missionary congregation. No, the missionary church retains all the essentials of the church, but it puts mission at the top of its agenda. Now it is right to ask what being a missionary church entails beyond simply growing numerically and we shall return to this question later. Suffice it to say we shall need structures which reflect this new way of 'being church.'

We can learn something from the structures of the early missionary churches. There are the lessons to be learnt from those of other eras and from different continents, where the church has been in the minority, for as Robert Warren reminds us, the church in "mission mode" is 'set in a culture where a number of competing value systems and worldviews exist alongside each other. Such is the present setting of the church…This is why we need a missionary church.'[5]

What Will Happen?

I am just old enough to know that of all organisations, the Church of England will not rush into anything, so do not panic! But in reality it has got to speed up—or there will be nothing left to keep going.

When churches at various times in history have embarked on missionary activity in a neighbouring or foreign culture, they have seen their task in terms of creating missionary congregations which would constantly reproduce themselves. They were set up to birth new churches continually. What we are seeking to do now is to embark upon a similar kind of missionary strategy for ourselves. It will involve taking our congregations, who largely hold different values, through a change process. This task is difficult. Some believe it cannot be done. They quote from the parables of Jesus to suggest that the old wineskins have to be jettisoned and new ones created. History will tell us whether that proves to be the case.

The Diocese of Wakefield has led the way here and titled itself 'The Missionary Diocese of Wakefield' to express its vision for mission. Every province, diocese, individual parish and congregation in the Church of England is now faced with a challenge: 'Are you prepared to redefine your vision and modify your structures in order to become a missionary province, diocese or congregation?' (Whether or not individual dioceses modify their titles is a secondary issue.)

The importance of this paradigm shift is widely recognized and different traditions are convinced by appropriate arguments. And I perceive that there is a remarkable convergence of thinking in people from almost all streams within the Church of England that something needs to be done. The outworking of this will, like all true missionary work, be dictated by the local situation—housing, work and leisure patterns, and current religious norms.

---

5   Robert Warren, *op cit*, p 3.

2

Meeting the Culture

There are a number of vital issues connected with the emerging culture of our day, which lead us to consider various aspects of the missionary congregation.

In particular, there is the need for the church to engage with contemporary culture. Robert Warren makes clear that the difference between a pastoral and a missionary church

'...is the difference between a church organized around sustaining, developing and promoting its own life, and a church organized around participating in God's mission in the world to establish his redemptive purposes in the whole of human life. A working definition of a missionary congregation is thus:

A missionary congregation is a church which takes its identity, priorities, and agenda, from participation in God's mission in the world.'[6]

You may prefer the term 'emerging' to 'missionary.' Robert Warren has increasingly used the term 'inherited' to describe the current maintenance/pastoral orientation of the church and 'emerging' to describe the church of the future. This avoids laying on the missionary congregation unhelpful overtones from the past. On the other hand the term 'emerging church' could be filled with almost any kind of meaning you care to lay on it. So I shall go on using 'missionary' for now, but try and put out of your mind pith helmets and so forth.

Culture

The missionary church over the centuries has much to teach us, not least the need to be responsive to the needs of the surrounding culture—sometimes challenging it, sometimes building on it, always listening to it. This was the way the Celtic missionaries operated in Britain.[7] It is why a town on the South coast of England is planting a congregation in the deanery for people of 'Radio 1 culture.' We live in a society of many different subcultures.

However, there are some common features of contemporary culture which are important for church people to grasp. They may help to explain why many today find the church so culturally inappropriate. For example, think of someone you know who is under twenty five, and check these values with them in mind.

- A distrust of institutions.
- Relationships based on personal encounter not established hierarchy.
- A preference for the informal rather than the formal.
- A desire for personal fulfilment and purpose—the cult of the individual.

6 Robert Warren, *op cit,* p 4.
7 See Michael Mitton, *Restoring the Woven Cord* (London: DLT, 1995).

- Variety—a great fear of boredom.
- Concern with immediate fulfilment and personal gratification.
- Future- not past-oriented.
- Customers who want value for money.
- People who want to be entertained.

To many such people the church seems to be locked in an almost impenetrable culture of its own, making the gospel inaccessible to them. Church members and clergy too, find the inherited mode of being church is simply a hindrance—not a help—in their work and ministry. The following typical remarks illustrate this.

From the unchurched who recognize a considerable cultural gap between themselves and the church:
- It is irrelevant to my life.
- I have never been.
- You do not need to go to church to be a Christian.
- The church is outdated.
- The church is corrupt—like the monarchy and politicians.
- Surviving is hard enough without being made to feel guilty.

From church members who find the church hinders not helps their witness:
- The mark of a committed Christian in our church is the number of meetings you attend for the church every week.
- At work I am a somebody, at church I am nobody.
- At work I am a nobody, at church I am somebody.
- I have given up trying to relate Christianity to work.
- I suppose I would like to 'blow the whistle' on certain things at work, but it is too risky.
- I keep church and work in compartments. People at work do not know I go to church and people at church do not realize what I do at work.
- I make sure my friends at school do not know I go to church. They would think I am weird.

From clergy who feel that the way we do church does not fit their vision of ministry:
- I have to spend far too much time on administration. If only I could get on with the real job.
- No one trained me in church planting or running *Alpha* groups, and the Archdeacon or the Bishop are far too busy with their administration to help with that kind of thing.
- My greatest headache is buildings. Without the problems of buildings we could get on with the job.

You can make up your own list I am sure, which will reflect your particular situations in town, city or countryside. However, what the church members and ministers are talking about here are not the kind of problems which might be dismissed as part of life in a healthy local church. These are distressed cries from the heart. Here is a church in crisis. While many of these are, I am happy to say, problems of growth, overall the church is still not experiencing numerical growth.

The message from the secular public is that the church is largely irrelevant, and some people in the church may feel the same. Perhaps it is not too surprising that, overall, fewer and fewer people are coming to church. The difficulties the church faces are that culture is both in transition and is diverse.

Since culture is in transition, there are few commonly held values. Institutions are regarded with suspicion for having mixed motives. People talk of being postmodern, which simply means the era after this one. There is a lack of a sense of where we are heading. The church has hardly caught up with the modern era, it is also one of the institutions regarded with suspicion. Yet if we could recapture the pioneering Spirit of the missionary church, perhaps we could yet have an authentic voice.

But culture is diverse—there is no longer a single culture. Even in a discrete community age differences raise profound barriers. The hope of a classless society has been lost in a whirlwind of diverse and independent groupings. The church cannot minister effectively by expecting everyone to join a single congregation. In future local churches will need multiple congregations, some meeting on weekdays.

3

In Search of Becoming a Missionary Church

Faced with an inherited way of 'being church,' which is hampering mission rather than enabling it, what are we to do? There have been missions and evangelistic events. However, 'up front' evangelists have sometimes assumed that everyone else can do what they do with a bit more courage. This kind of gift projection has been unhelpful. Most Christians do evangelism by drawing people into the faith community, rather than giving them a personal course in Christianity. This means that the faith community must itself be the primary agent *of mission.* We will always need those with the gift of bringing faith to birth, but the *church itself* must be missionary in outlook.

Do We Begin Again? The House Church Experience

But the institution seems ill-equipped to be outward facing. Should we abandon the institution and start again? The history of the house church movement is instructive here, for it might be argued that abandoning the institution and starting again was tried by the house church movement of the 1970s and 1980s.

Many people left mainline denominations to create congregations which they hoped would be mission-orientated but most of them became increasingly pastoral and maintenance-orientated. This probably happened first because those who formed these new churches had just made a huge step in moving churches and they yearned for spiritual stability, and secondly, of course, because most of their leaders were people from that background. Thirdly, with a few exceptions, they were not founded primarily as missionary congregations but as alternative pastoral churches which had certain distinctive practices.

This lesson from recent history is particularly important for those engaged in planting a church or starting a new congregation. The natural tendency is to model a church plant on the predominantly pastoral mode of the 'mother' church, so perpetuating inherited ways of doing things.

It is important to say that recently some clusters of the 'new churches' have adopted a missionary congregation focus and some of these are the fastest growing churches in Britain.

Change or What?

The depth of our historical roots means that the Church of England has more momentum for continuing the inherited way of being church than perhaps any other denomination. Yet we have changed aspects of our corporate life and been seen to be adaptable when needed.

Before we go on I want to identify three areas relating to the institution which yield the most awkward obstacles to the change from maintenance to mission.

1. Buildings

Buildings are regarded by many as a most important aspect of the church which must be maintained at all costs. Yet most other organisations would move out of premises which have become a liability. Many churches do not feel that option is open to them. Most know that should the church burn down tomorrow, there would be little question but that it should be rebuilt, probably in a similar fashion.

Clearly, in some places the building might be an important part of being a missionary congregation, but the meeting place should never be the most important consideration. The church is a building of people (1 Peter 2.4,5). Buildings should serve the vision not vice versa. The early missionaries to Britain found that a building served the congregation well. It provided tangible evidence of intangible spiritual power. It was a kind of mark of the victory over paganism. Neither of these reasons seems appropriate today. Later generations, in pastoral mode, often used buildings as an expression of temporal power and influence of the kind that Jesus warned about.

Change needs to come, it seems to me, in the priorities and policy of the church. How does the *Maintenance to Mission* agenda affect the DAC (Diocesan Advisory Committee who deal with church buildings) for example? Has the vision of missionary congregations been taken on board by them? If so then for every submission the key question is whether this development serves the missionary vision. Furthermore, DACs have a responsibility to look out for abuse of temporal power and privilege in the business of buildings.

2. Finance and Staffing

The spiral of decline in some dioceses is frightening. If they pursue the policy of reducing stipendiary clergy, in the face of church growth principles, the income will go down and then yet more clergy will be removed. The church needs full-time paid ministers. Properly deployed they are vital for growing churches. First find your priests then the money will come. As Gavin Reid said recently, 'Pennies follow priests.'

There is a false argument here about lay ministry. For some feel that losing stipendiary ministers may facilitate lay ministry, and help put the church back into the hands of the members. It is not much comfort to lay people to know that they are doing it only because 'there is nobody else.' The missionary church needs more, not less, human resources and that includes, I have no doubt, full-time professionals and specialists and general practitioners. Indeed one of the marks of the early missionary church was the number and quality of those who gave their entire lives to the enterprise. They were full-time and more. I believe that long-term, the effectiveness of spare-timers depends on the number and competence of the full-timers who supervise them.

Ironically those dioceses which go the road of cutbacks rather than investment may in the end find themselves back on their feet financially sooner than others. But at a price. Diocesan authorities will find themselves left with a smaller number of financially viable units. Most of the churches left will be those which are growing and where giving is sacrificial and realistic. This will mark the end of the parish system as we know it.

The power and authority will rest fairly and squarely with the local congregations. Diocesan authority will diminish. Perhaps a sign of this will be when local churches ask the Bishop to choose from their three dates for the confirmation rather than the other way round, and Synod will decide whether or not to appoint another Archdeacon.

A missionary diocese will acknowledge that some areas will bear fruit less quickly than others. It will expect every parish to contribute to the missionary enterprise. It will create 'mission priority areas.' It will help those parishes where buildings are sapping energy and finances by sharing the responsibility for those structures considered appropriate for the missionary purpose.

3. Liturgy

What does the missionary church require? Does it need liturgy at all? Is liturgy a feature of a church which we no longer are? Should we put our liturgy in cold storage and wait until a later date to defrost it? Or will the emerging church perhaps bring us a renewal of liturgy?

For many church people, the point at which change begins to hurt, or at least be uncomfortable, is when the services change, and this usually involves the liturgy. Yet liturgy provides a core of worship material which is known and prayed. As the 1662 prayer book aimed to do, it needs to be in the language of the people—in other words indigenous.

With the revision of the Alternative Service Book in prospect and equipped with *Worship and the Word*, where do we go from here? My own view is that the ASB did not indigenize the liturgy for the modern era; it was simply a necessary expedient in the transition from a liturgy for the church in pastoral mode to a liturgy for the missionary era. Inevitably different missionary congregations will develop new liturgies or adapt established ones. Liturgy in its broadest sense must be appropriate. But why does it need to be in a written code? Increasingly the communication language of our time is multimedia. Perhaps liturgists in five hundred years will speak with equal reverence about Gutenburg and Silicon Valley. Hopefully the next ASB will appear on multi media CD ROM. A key benefit of previous liturgies has been that good and valuable material has been made available to everyone. Expertise can be shared. This principle of finding the best and disseminating it for others to use is important. Resources need to be invested in central databases of material from a variety of media which can be accessed by the smallest congregation.

The principles behind liturgy are about enabling corporate worship and unifying around an agreed pattern of prayer, praise and discovery. These are values which God's people have found sustaining in their spiritual lives down the centuries. Postmodern liturgy must make its own contribution to this rich tradition.

4
Building Blocks of the
New Missionary Congregations

I want to introduce a number of initiatives which may help us turn our congregations round. They are like pieces in the jigsaw of the new missionary movement. Changing the metaphor, one of these may be for you the first building block of a new kind of church. As you will see, a number of these developments are not intrinsically new, but the fact that they are being considered at this time is a measure of the degree of seriousness with which the church is searching for ways forward. One could also say that under God, these initiatives have been nurtured and have proved themselves so they are now ready for wider distribution at a point when we so desperately need models of missionary congregations.

Church Planting: Our Best Chance of Working From First Principles
The church planting movement is now facing the question: 'What kind of church are we planting?' For here is the opportunity above all others to model for the rest of the church a missionary congregation. The difficulty is that it is very hard for people whose only experience of church is 'pastoral' to plant a different kind of church.

I believe the church planting movement is at a vital cross roads. It is our best chance to get missionary congregations up and running. However, I know of no identifiable trend that is marking out new church plants in this way.

Willow Creek: The First of a New Wave of Missionary Congregations
The most important and, I believe, the long-term impact of Willow Creek Community Church in Chicago is not their precise model ('Seeker Services') but their tenacity of purpose. I said at the end of my introduction to this church that, '...if the church in the UK really begins to adopt a "missionary" rather than a pastoral stance, prioritizing the lost rather than the found, and if this is reflected in both recruitment and training, financial provision and Spiritual resources, then perhaps the Decade will make the kind of impact so many readers of this booklet have been hoping and praying for.'[8]

What Willow Creek brings us is not a model but a message. Here is a church which can truly claim to be a missionary congregation, because it has put mission at the top of the agenda. When they have a building project, they ask how it serves the unchurched. When they appoint a staff member they want to know what contact she or he has with those outside, and what commitment they have

---

8 Paul Simmonds, *Reaching the Unchurched: Some Lessons from Willow Creek* (Grove Evangelism Series No 19, Grove Books, 1992) p 23.

to the missionary vision. This is a church which has not needed to move from maintenance to mission—it started out that way seventeen years ago as a small congregation.

Alternative Services: The Forerunner of the Missionary Congregation

While Willow Creek was getting the headlines, there were other people here in the UK who were busy experimenting, especially in the area of the emerging youth culture. The key features of these alternative services were that they were linked to a particular culture whether rave, teenage or twenties. The number and range of these groups has been steadily growing, and some have formed loose networks. *Holy Disorder* now has a magazine linking groups and a training roadshow. It has many of the marks of the new style way of being church described by Robert Warren. Many are run by young people themselves. Few have strong institutional ties. Suffice it to say that it does not take a genius to work out that this kind of church and the world of quotas and synods are culturally miles apart. The Nine O'clock Service community had been courageously encouraged by the Bishop and others, and did an important work for many years while a congregation attached to a traditional evangelical church.[9]

These are new congregations. They are effectively church plants. They are one of our best hopes of establishing a bridgehead in some cultures which are otherwise virtually unreached by the Christian gospel. The begin by asking questions about the concerns and needs of that cultural group. And like all good missionary work, the resulting ministry is a response to the identified needs of that group.

Toronto: The New Missionary Movement's Pentecost?

Robert Warren makes much of the need for a church to be clear about its spirituality, which provides the divine energy and direction to be a new church for a new age. I am personally fascinated by the thought that just as the Spirit came in obvious and life renewing manifestations before the launch of the first missionary movement, so almost out of the blue we have a fresh outpouring of the Spirit at this time. This has been dubbed the Toronto blessing because of its geographical origins.

Of course there are problems, but we need to be mature and experienced enough to take these in our stride—after all, it is at least twenty years since we began to talk about charismatic renewal. In some ways, I think this is a reminder that a missionary church, above all others, confronts principalities and powers. One of the pieces of liturgy which has come from the first missionary age and has passed through the pastoral age unchanged is the parents' renunciation of evil and the bidding to fight the devil, which are part of the baptism service.

---

9   The tragic take-over of NOS by New Age influences undermined the theology and ethics of its former leader. This does not mean that similar initiatives should be closed. It does mean that we may need to find new structures which will be more appropriate in supporting similar future manifestations of the missionary church.

Adult Catechumenate and the Journey of Faith, Alpha and Cursillo

In the past ten years there has been a new emphasis on the journey of faith. There has been a growth in interest in the Adult Catechumenate. Robert Warren comments on the danger of a kind of evangelism which focuses on an initial encounter but has no depth. There has been increasing use of longer-term courses and the emphasis on a journey into faith in both catholic and evangelical traditions. Thus we saw pioneering churches running 'Christian Foundations' 'Agnostics Anonymous' and so on during the eighties. This trickle became a stream when CPAS Christian Basics appeared at the turn of the decade, and it has become a torrent with the arrival of *Alpha*.

Alpha is very interesting for a number of reasons. First, to some extent it appeals to the enlightenment culture, which is still a significant part of many people's world view. Second, it combines traditional apologetics with Cursillo-type experiential weekends with their emphasis on the Spirit's work.[10] Third, it is being run in a variety of churches, large and small. Some present the material in the 'Seeker Service' anonymous way, others in more informal, even homely, settings.

Meta-church: Ministry for a Nineties Culture

How do you provide a structure of church life which can cope with rapid growth? Most English churches would not know what to do, if they experienced sudden substantial growth in numbers. The writings of Carl George have recently excited a number of churches in Britain and the US for he has international experience of missionary congregations. His books, including *Prepare your Church for the Future* (Revell), are strongly in the church growth tradition, although he wants to modify parts of that. He has called this emerging way of working *meta-church*. In particular he looks again at the three classical levels of church life coined by the church growth people: cell; congregation; celebration. He suggests we should concentrate on two of these, the cell and celebration. The cell is the foundation. It can reproduce rapidly and provide a place for new Christians to be nurtured and cared for.

Interestingly enough, Willow Creek, who have nothing akin to the congregation size group, have more recently started to regard small groups as essential for every member. Everyone is asked to belong to a self-reproducing (missionary) small group or cell. It is noteworthy that the largest church in the world, in Korea with Pastor Paul Yonggi Cho, is also organized around small groups and their leaders. Many of Carl George's ideas have their roots in the cell church movement. Like other initiatives mentioned here, this has been around for some years. The books of Ralph Neighbour and Robert Banks were published in the eighties, yet their models are highly relevant for the emerging church today.[11]

---

10 Cursillo started as a lay movement following the death of many priests in the Spanish revolution. Its Anglican expression preserves the elements of a long renewal weekend away and regular meetings in cells and clusters of cells, aimed at deepening spiritual life.

11 See Ralph Neighbour, *Where do We Go from Here?* (Houston, Texas: Torch, 1990).

The Cell Church Model

Why is the cell church so important for the missionary congregation concept? It enables every member to participate in mission. The cell church movement regards cells as missionary. Carl George suggests that each group has an empty chair to encourage people to bring friends. Ralph Neighbour expects each group to birth a new group within a specified period, say eighteen months. The apprentice leader knows from the outset that they will be leading the new group. This arrangement for small groups is strikingly missionary in emphasis. Now most traditional house groups would find such a transition rather difficult. Changing priorities from pastoral to missionary always is. There is a cost too in terms of personal comfort. Probably the way forward is to adopt the vision of birthing when the groups are reconstituted after a break. Or it may be possible to begin with one or two new groups, or ask for groups to volunteer to pioneer this approach. Cell churches usually operate with coordinating leaders over every five home groups. This is arranged so that everyone in a leadership role is supervised and meets with other leaders for mutual accountability and support. For a church to expand rapidly, there must be a way of producing leaders quickly.

A New Training Paradigm—VHS

Carl George points out that the church in the West has a model of training which consists of maximum initial training (often theoretical) and minimal ongoing support. This is of course largely true of clergy training but the same values are passed on in our training of lay people. So whether it is a diocese or parachurch agency the tendency has been to provide hefty training sessions but minimal follow-up support. Missionary culture turns this on its head. There is neither the time nor the resources to do high initial training—and it is not what is needed. So initial training will be low but with a high level of ongoing training and support. This, of course, was Jesus' way of training his disciples and has been well proven by various traditions ever since—from the Religious Orders to the Navigators.

Carl George suggests that, to be effective, house group leaders' support should be provided fortnightly. This is much more frequent than most British churches would consider necessary, but it is needed for effective coaching and regular skills training. He also rates highly the place of vision and offers a powerful way of ensuring continuous and effective support by combining the three elements of skill training, coaching (huddle), and vision. He calls it the VHS agenda: Vision, Huddle, Skill. The key support a small group leader needs is a fortnightly meeting with an agenda of Vision, Huddle and Skill. In a church with up to five groups, the minister would lead the VHS meeting, attended by five leaders and five assistant leaders. In a larger church the support is 'cascaded down.'

Vision needs to be on every agenda—either to be expounded or to be modified. An experienced minister said to me recently that the more he looked around at the needs of churches the more he realized that vision is vitally important—especially, I would add, in a period of cultural upheaval. Perhaps 'vision casting' was not exactly the key attribute required by the vicar of a small 17th century village where everybody attended church. But today vision is key. As I pondered this, I thought how often I had seen churches and people lose their way for lack of vision. I pondered the number of organist-vicar disagreements which stemmed, not from personality differences, but because there was no agreed vision to work to. Vision clarifies purpose and allows us to say, 'It may be important but not for now.' Thus we are released from the tyranny of 'Let's try to keep everybody happy' which subconsciously is the ultimate hope of many vicars.

Huddle. Secondly, priority is given to on-going support. This is done by encouraging feedback and helping each other, perhaps by working in sub groups. In order for feedback to work it must happen soon after the event. So effective support must be regular and frequent. Small group leaders can talk about problems in their group. There can be prayer and planning, and sharing of ideas.

Skill is the third element. The growing of skills is, as we have seen, on-going. This is where the regular on-the-job training comes in, more in the form of coaching. Most training materials on the market are modular, so you do not overload people. They have time to try out a new way of praying or a fresh approach to study. Recently in our average-sized church we have introduced a VHS meeting. We meet fortnightly alternately with the house groups. We have made use of various skill training approaches, including using the CPAS course 'Growing Groups.' One group leader described it as the most useful meeting he attended.

A number of British churches have been trying the VHS model, with considerable success. Steve Croft in Halifax has added 'Ministry,' and varies the emphasis from meeting to meeting—but he has not found a better acronym! Another church prefers Vision, Action (or Application) and Training —VAT for short.

The Cell Church: A Good Way to Begin?

The 'cell church' movement obviously has parallels with church planting. Church planting might equally be called church birthing. For many churches, the cell church model may well be their best chance for becoming a missionary church on the grounds that small groups are more flexible than congregations. With a congregation you have no choice but to go through a period of transition. With groups you can at least begin with new groups, with a new lease of life and a new set of values.

Church Growth Study: The Discipline Behind Missionary Congregations

We have much to learn from students of church growth, in particular the importance of full-time staff. For example, it is a well documented phenomenon in England that a church grows up to a maximum of 100—200 per full time staff member and then overload sets in. Yet there seems no mechanism in the dioceses to monitor growth and as soon as that number is reached to trigger an appropriate response. This might include a training programme, some coaching and or even a team coming in from another church which has broken through to a new size. Ideally, extra full or part time help would be put in. But the Church of England seems incapable of talking about success in terms of numbers and is even more reluctant to invest more clergy in successful churches, for fear of a backlash of some kind. A lot of churches therefore reach their ceiling and 'bounce off,' sometimes into decline.

People drop out unnoticed from the church or find themselves in a pastoral vacuum. This has been called the revolving door syndrome. Others are simply not reaching their full potential as followers of Christ. Our current ways of working mean that most of the work is done by the faithful few. There needs to be a revolution in church life, where the centre of gravity moves from the congregation to the small group. In the congregation, ministry is seen as the responsibility of the few; in the cell, every member shares the responsibility for the effectiveness or otherwise of the cell.[12] This enables everybody to become involved. The cell must be community based and set free to be the church in microcosm.

Ministry: Let Us Change

It is to be hoped that the Advisory Board of Ministry (ABM) look with the eyes of the Lambeth conference to the needs of the church in the next century, or we may find ourselves as a missionary church without missionaries. We may have missionary congregations but the only ordained leaders around will be those selected and trained for a situation which has passed. In addition to a whole range of church planters, we will require church leaders whose primary task is to grow and birth churches, manage mega-churches and work at the frontiers of the established church. John Tiller suggests we need a new apostolic ministry with a roving dimension.[13]

Hopefully there can be a new mission emphasis in the stated selection criteria. Meanwhile, the interpretation of these criteria is in the hands of the selectors—Bishop's selectors. Will the Bishops increasingly choose people who are 'missionary' rather than 'pastorally' inclined? As far as existing clergy are concerned, I think many will demand a crash course to fit them for ministry in the emerging church. But there will also be a need to help congregations through change, and that is where an interregnum or sabbatical might help.

The Interregnum and Sabbaticals: Windows of Opportunity?

An interregnum could be an opportunity for a team to assess the parish and ensure that the new appointment moves the church forward. There are dioceses here and in the US where a diocesan team takes the parish through a period of reorientation and change. The new incumbent can then take them on from that point, leading them into a new vision. For churches not anticipating changing their vicar, a process could be developed which included, say, a three month sabbatical for the minister to be based in a 'mission-orientated' church. During the

---

12 A network of these groups, started by Ian Freestone, a Church Army chaplain in Balgowlah, Australia, includes being a 'change-agent' in the community and providing for the poor as additional goals.

13 See John Tiller, *Tiller Ten Years On* (Grove Pastoral Series No 55, Nottingham: Grove Books, 1993).

sabbatical the congregation would be helped to change their expectations and start using different structures.

Advertising and the Media: Come Back—All is Forgiven!

In 1945, the report *Towards the Conversion of England'* recommended that the church spend over a million pounds over five years, (then a huge sum) on a publicity campaign. This, I think, was a remarkably prophetic thought. Until recently, the church relied entirely on publicity through the news media. The net result is that the good news never gets out, only the bad. Long ago, other groupings realized that this is at best unpredictable and at worst means that you only get adverse publicity which can undermine years of patient work. The church has begun to embark on an advertising programme. I believe that the church cannot avoid the need to have a continuous flow of positive press and advertising output.

Christian Broadcasting: Cheers and Boos?

There are still those who, in the traditions of public service broadcasting, want the Christian faith included but would not want it to be in any way proselytizing. The roots of these values are in the post war era when the BBC had monopoly of the airwaves. Interestingly this was precisely the time when *Towards the Conversion of England* was shelved for promoting the Christian faith in a 'vulgar' commercial way. The church was for once ahead of the game if it could have but known it. Now commercial broadcasting is in the ascendancy, Christians either go in with a purpose or abandon it to others.

Technology

Technology is ushering in a whole new world. Take, for instance, the internet. You plug a phone line into your computer instead of a printer, and someone the other side of the world gets your document on their screen. On the internet the only barrier is language, and that problem will soon be solved with automated translation of documents. You can call up material from 'sites' such as colleges, companies and individuals on almost any subject. For example, there is an Australian 'address' for those who want to 'discuss,' by exchanging messages, the emergence of cell churches referred to above.[14]

'Go into all the world and preach the gospel' has now taken on a new dimension. You can engage in 'conversation' evangelism from the comfort of your computer keyboard, with someone the other side of the world. There is huge potential for international youth evangelism (the majority of internet users are under twenty). In one diocese, an enterprising youth officer has put up a poster which simply has an e-mail address. Unchurched young people connect out of curiosity.

Let's take this further. Thousands of clergy up and down the country spend upwards of 20% of their time preparing materials for services and sermons. Why not have a specialist group to do the bulk of that preparation, introducing a de-

---

14 Site address: cell-church-request@bible.acu.edu

gree of excellence and expertise which local spirituality and creativity cannot match, and distribute it via internet, phone line, video link, satellite or whatever means is cost effective? After all, using locally a widely available resource is not a new idea, not even in 1662!

Lambeth: The Official Starting Gun

There may be cynicism in some quarters about the relevance of a gathering of Bishops at the ancient seat of Lambeth. But public image aside, the meeting of international heads of Anglican churches was well placed to offer an objective and unequivocal analysis of that part of the church which includes the Church of England. The message from the Bishops in 1988 said: 'This conference calls for a shift to a dynamic missionary emphasis going beyond care and nurture to proclamation and service.'[15]

5

Four Insights, Three Steps and a Final Reflection

How Do You Become a Missionary Congregation?

This is a key question, for which there are few answers. I hope it is clear now that a missionary congregation is not a pastoral congregation with evangelistic connections, it is a pastoral church turned inside out:

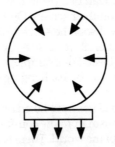 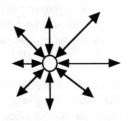

A pastoral church   *A missionary church*
which does evangelism

Running a pastoral church which does evangelism is like transporting petrol by loading drums on a truck. It can achieve a little, but how much better if you had a proper tanker designed for the job. A missionary church is designed for the job.

---

15 Lambeth Conference, 1988.

Four Insights

One of the crucial principles which has emerged from various quarters is the importance of *vision*. In the past some leaders have had a private vision and managed their church to an agenda which was not shared. This is a recipe for demotivation with people pulling in different directions. It may of course take a long time—years—for the new vision of the missionary church to be established in the bloodstream of a congregation and even longer before it is understood by the parish.

This leads to the second observation: you may have to *start small* with a group or cell within the congregation. Bringing about change in a church is a complex task. There is a training need here for ministers.

Thirdly, one of the best ways to introduce change in an Anglican setting, according to many clergy, is to set up *experiments*. This demonstrates that the change is provisional and most people find it easier if they have understood and can see its effects.

Fourthly, the principle of *multiple congregations* and multiple groups must not only be accepted but actively pursued. Hardly any clergy now are in the position of running one service a week for one group of people from just one culture. Most supervise a number of different congregations and small groups. Clergy have to work out ways of relating to these groups and the groups need to work out ways of relating to each other.

Three Steps

So what are the key steps to begin the process of creating a missionary congregation?

First, put mission at the top of the agenda. This is probably the most difficult. Becoming a missionary congregation is acknowledged to be a paradigm shift.

- If you are church planting you can declare your priority from the beginning.
- If you are a minister moving to a new job you may be also in a position to effect change and from the start set up leadership patterns commensurate with missionary congregation status.
- If the church is settled it may be that you need to begin with one house group who are prepared to put mission first—committed to birth a new group within, say, a year or eighteen months.
- It may be that nobody in the congregation shares your vision and all you can do is try and get people to understand the need to move in a new direction. Do not worry about the detail of the vision. That comes later. In the matter of change direction is key.

Second, translate that priority into a vision statement. This is important. It must be short and memorable and it must have mission at the top. (Some people inevitably will fault this as being too rigorous, too idealistic. But it is a tool. The test, it seems to me, is whether the church gets into the habit of prioritizing and planning according to the needs of the unchurched. A vision statement helps to ensure this.)

Third, identify the culture of those you are concerned for. This may be the immediate community or it may be the network of contacts of Christians. John Clarke has identified a number of different 'fringe' communities.[16] These include the people we live with, our neighbours, people we work with and people with whom we pursue our hobbies. However, the kingdom must permeate beyond our fringes, unless we are to abandon great sections of our society.

The target group will vary from church to church. For example, one church identified young people as the culture they needed to focus on. Another had already been working with unchurched elderly people, and so put all their efforts into developing a 'seeker' service for them.

Time to Turn

At the beginning I said that there were probably three reasons for the failure of the church to put itself into missionary mode in 1945. First, the institution of the church was not prepared to change. Secondly, the church was cushioned from reality by the inherited financial resources of the church. Thirdly, people wanted a pastoral church to shield them from the changes in society. I hope that none of these will hinder us this time. Financially, the church can no longer rely on inherited resources. I think future generations may give thanks for the Church Commissioners' losses! There is, however, the sheer inertia of the pastoral church, which will be hard to overcome. Indeed, Robert Warren likens it to a huge oil tanker which cannot be stopped quickly, but it can be turned to take a new direction. And it only takes a relatively small tug to do it.

If the Church of England is to emerge as a growing vibrant church, it is going to have to go through this 'paradigm shift.' Such change brings bereavement for the past and fear for the future, and for some, great excitement. As with any change, there will be some at the leading edge who have already stopped reading this booklet because it is not radical enough. There will be some who do not want change. If you are one of them, perhaps you feel like those who in 1945 wanted the church to provide a degree of stability.

If you do not feel you can cope with this kind of change at this time (and until I have survived a few years in it, who am I to criticize?), ask your minister to set aside a congregation for people like you which will take care of your spiritual needs. All that will be asked of you is that the congregation is self sufficient and makes as few demands as possible on the rest of the church. You can make use of the building at times when the missionary congregations do not need it. But please, for the sake of those outside, do not take any more resources than you have to. More positively, you may like to pledge support for some of the missionary congregations which you know. When the West is won, we shall turn to you for the model of a pastoral church once more.[17] I think, in fact, that most Christians will

---

16 John Clarke, *Evangelizing the Fringe* (Grove Evangelism booklet 30, 1995) and *Evangelism that Really Works* (London: SPCK, 1995).

17 Martin Robinson, *To Win the West* (Crowborough, E Sussex: Monarch 1995).

find the process of transformation a little uncomfortable at times, but will warm to their task and as they find a new appreciation of the gospel and will become more comfortable about sharing it with their friends.

The importance of the missionary purpose of the people of God was firmly recognized, in 1945, in paragraph 85 of the ·Towards the Conversion of England report which quotes William Temple: 'The primary purpose for which the Spirit is given is that we may bear witness to Christ. We must not expect the gift while we ignore the purpose. A church which ceases to be missionary will not be, and cannot rightly expect to be "spiritual."'[18]

A Final Reflection

In his first book Robert Warren suggests that we need to start *Building Missionary Congregations*. His second book, *Being Human, Being Church*, is far more detailed and exploratory about how a missionary congregation might begin.

Robert Warren set out by using the terms *pastoral* and *mission* mode and ended up using the terms *inherited* and *emerging*. My outlook is inevitably strongly coloured by my inherited church background which many Grove readers will share. One of the weaknesses of the inherited mode of church life is that it has functioned as though there were only one right way of doing things. A church in mission mode will instead be shaped by its context and marked by diversity. Although I have described what I think some missionary congregations might look like, I am inevitably using the terms of our inherited way of doing things.

What Robert Warren has done is to show that the missionary church of the future needs to take the contemporary world seriously. He also makes clear his belief that:
1. The missionary church needs to be sustainable in a changing environment.
2. The missionary church needs to be more than a recruiting church dedicated to increasing numbers.

Any *growing* church must be alert to the nature and extent of that growth. Using the inherited way of talking, we would say that St Agatha's has grown by 100 members. But unless these people are committed to the same values of the Kingdom as the rest of us, we are simply building a church of converts not Christians, of devotees not disciples. That is an ever present risk.

Danger One: Loveless Evangelism

This raises the question of the nature of the missionary congregation. It is at this point that it might be possible to misunderstand Robert Warren, for he is uneasy about Emil Brunner's famous phrase, 'The church exists by mission as a fire by burning.' The word *mission*, he argues, should be replaced by love. I think this is probably the comment of someone with the ability to see beyond the immediate radical numerical growth required now to the church of the future. When Bill Hybels came to Britain in 1992 he spoke of the vision at Willow Creek

---

18 William Temple, *Readings in St John* (Macmillan, 1945) p 386.

(sustained for fifteen years) to 'turn irreligious people into fully devoted followers of Christ.' Interestingly, in 1994, he spoke of the spiritual pilgrimage of the church in the intervening two years when increasingly they had discovered the importance of what he called 'love of another kind.' Some of us wondered for a while what had happened to the priority of mission. It was there and still at the top of the agenda, but it was tagged with the reminder that especially in a missionary congregation 'if I have not love I am...a clanging cymbal' (1 Cor 13).

I suspect that this is a journey most of us make. There are many motivations for putting mission first. But having put mission first, we will soon find that sustainable mission is only possible when God's love permeates his people. Missionary work which loses its love becomes colonialism. It is not difficult to see examples in history and even now of churches where there is loveless evangelizing. Paul recognized that this was inevitable, with some preaching Christ from envy, as he told the Philippians (Phil 1.15).

Enthusiasm is not enough. Any missionary training establishment will tell you that the excitement of the missionary challenge is insufficient of itself to sustain the motivation; there has to be a deep underlying love. The body of Christ needs head as well as heart, energy as well as emotion.

Should we therefore remove numerical growth from our vision because of the risk of loveless evangelism? Bill Hybels spoke about 'love of another kind' in the context of a constant stream of unchurched people finding that love for themselves. There is no authentic Christian love unless it is shared.

Danger Two: Love Without Evangelism

I also want to make clear in this booklet my conviction that simply creating a more loving Christian community is not sufficient if that means we simply work harder at making ourselves more comfortable. My greatest temptation is to make church an extension of my comfort zone. That will not do.

So the concept of the missionary congregation faces two great dangers: evangelism without love and love without evangelism. What we are called to is evangelism with love from the church.

Perhaps the last word should go to a great missionary practitioner Henry Martyn:

'The Spirit of Christ is the spirit of missions, and the nearer we get to him the more intensely missionary we must become.'